For Finnegan

NICK DEAR

The Dark Earth and the Light Sky

faber and faber

First published in 2012
by Faber and Faber Ltd
74–77 Great Russell Street
London WC1B 3DA

Typeset by Country Setting, Kingsdown, Kent CT14 8ES
Printed in England by CPI Bookmarque, Croydon, Surrey

A CIP record for this book
is available from the British Library

ISBN 978–0–571–29075–8

2 4 6 8 10 9 7 5 3 1

The Dark Earth and the Light Sky was first presented at the Almeida Theatre, London, on 8 November 2012. The cast, in alphabetical order, was as follows:

Edward Thomas Pip Carter
Eleanor Farjeon Pandora Colin
Philip Thomas Ifan Huw Dafydd
Robert Frost Shaun Dooley
Helen Thomas Hattie Morahan
Bott / Major Lushington Dan Poole

Director Richard Eyre
Design Bob Crowley
Lighting Peter Mumford
Sound and Music John Leonard
Casting Cara Beckinsale
Dialect Jill McCullough

Characters

Edward Thomas

Helen Thomas

Robert Frost

Eleanor Farjeon

Philip Thomas

Arnold Bott

Major Franklin Lushington

THE DARK EARTH AND THE LIGHT SKY

Act One

SCENE ONE

1910. Deep in Hampshire. Edward Thomas, in his early thirties, wiry and intense, enters at a brisk pace, with a stout stick and a knapsack.

His wife Helen, a year older, becomes visible. Edward doesn't see her, but she watches him.

Helen (*to us*) The question everyone asks is, why? Why would he, why did he, why? And I have tried to answer it but oh. People do strange things, don't they? Edward especially. I don't know why he did what he did. All I know is, he was *mine*.

Edward pauses, listens. He can hear birdsong. Helen hears it too. Edward pulls a notebook and pencil from his pocket.

(*To us.*) It's only a linnet. But he'll write down the date and the time and the map reference. And the cloud formations and where he stopped for lunch. Christ.

Edward makes his notes.

Walking, walking, walking. What's wrong with a bus or a train? But no, he'd rather tramp. He refers me to Hazlitt and Coleridge and Defoe, and when I've time I take a look, but to be honest I haven't much time. Not now. In the old days, though, when he brought me books, when my lover brought me literature . . .! I'd read!

Edward puts away his notebook and strides off.

I met Edward when I was seventeen and he was sixteen. He lived in Clapham and I lived in Wandsworth, and he became my dearest friend. We'd take long rambles, westwards out of town, talking, talking, teasing each other. I lost my virginity on my twentieth birthday – oh, with Edward of course! – in a thicket on Wimbledon Common. Which seemed to us a paradise. We were ignorant and innocent, and we loved each other very much. We didn't want a wedding – who needs a chit to be in love? – but oh, my mother, and oh, I was carrying Merfyn, she did go on, you'd think I'd done something indecent. I shouldn't give cheek but oh. So we married and moved to the country. From the start Edward was determined that all he would do was write. Which is fine if you start off from Bloomsbury, perhaps – or Paris, or Boston, or Rome – but not if you come from Clapham.

SCENE TWO

1911. Edward's father Philip is a fastidious man in a crisp suit with a wing collar. Edward enters with his briefcase, taking off his hat and coat.

Philip How was your train?

Edward Very busy.

Philip No delays?

Edward shakes his head.

How punctual was it?

Edward Very punctual.

Philip (*nods, pleased*) Your mother is getting your tea.

Edward I have something to say. I've made a decision. I know you won't like it but – I'm quitting.

Philip What do you mean, quitting? Quitting what?

Edward The Commission.

Philip The Commission?

Edward Yes.

Philip You have not been there three weeks.

Edward It isn't for me. I've resigned.

Philip It isn't for you?

Edward No.

A pause as Philip digests this terrible news.

Philip The Civil Service, not for you. Well, well.

Edward I'm sorry.

Philip Strings have been pulled, you know. Favours called in. It's not that easy to find a post in –

Edward I know. Thank you for everything you've –

Philip And in time you will get out and about. Surely you can see it's the ideal position for a –

Edward It seems I would be stuck in London rather more than we had thought. It is an office job, Father.

Philip But you are no clerk in a basement, you are high-level, you are Assistant Secretary to the Royal Commission on Ancient Monuments –

Edward It's an office job.

Philip Now, yes, *now*, but in due course you will be out there, sketching the cairns and the standing stones, across all of Wales and Monmouthshire, just as you desired –

Edward I desired to live in the country, not –

Philip Yes, in the country, I know, but –

Edward I find myself lodging with my parents, and travelling up to town: Clapham Junction, every morning, eight-fifteen.

Philip And your weekends are your own. Edward, you are approaching middle age.

Edward I thought I could commute from Hampshire. But it's impossible. Helen is wretched. I've given my notice.

Philip Well, you are several kinds of fool.

Edward So you've told me, Father.

Philip Do you know what this is reminding me of? This is reminding me of the day you threw the walking race at school.

Edward I did not throw the walking race at school.

Philip You were in the lead, and you stopped! What is that then? You threw the race!

Edward I was frightened.

Philip Frightened of what?

Edward Winning, I suppose.

Philip (*with a weary sigh*) Edward, sit down.

Edward sits.

I am sure that it must have come as a shock, going to work. I expect your collar is uncomfortable, your tea break unfathomably short. But these are accommodations men must make. You have children. Mouths to feed. You cannot dislike everything for ever.

Edward I don't dislike everything.

Philip You complain about everything.

Edward That's different, that's a critical evaluation of –

Philip I started with nothing, in Tredegar. And look at us now, in a villa – brand new.

Edward It's a semi-detached.

Philip It's a villa. To our people in Wales, we are kings, we live like kings. For this I have sacrificed my Mondays, Tuesdays, Wednesdays, Thursdays and Fridays for forty years and odd. And my weekends, they are my own. This is what we call 'making a living'; was it never mentioned at Oxford?

Edward I can still make a living at reviewing –

Philip Writing, that is scarcely a job –

Edward With respect, Father, I have been a published writer since I was eighteen –

Philip – and there we have it. You would rather be a writer than provide for your family. Oh, what you could have been – what potential! A University man! But this cult of the countryside. This worship of turnips and greens. Cities, boyo! Cities are where men live, and do things. Here we are, at the beating heart of the greatest city ever known, and you'd rather live like a peasant, down in the Vale of Muck? Men improve themselves, that's what they do, men struggle to –

Edward But what have we improved?

Philip What?

Edward What is actually better than it was before?

Philip Why – everything!

Edward Everything? I remember when lavender was still grown on Lavender Hill. I remember when we could walk out through Tooting to open fields, and –

Philip Men fulfil their potential – they don't go backwards! Men fight for advancement, for schools, for housing, for unions, for the right to work!

Edward The right to work! What, are they too broken-spirited to dream of a right to *live*? I've had the right to work for three weeks, it's like being buried alive! I hate work, I despise it, it's pointless, I'd rather be dead!

SCENE THREE

Before the hearth in the Thomases' cottage at Steep, near Petersfield. Late at night. Helen sings softly as she rocks baby Myfanwy in her arms:

Helen

Blow the wind southerly, southerly, southerly
Blow the wind south o'er the bonnie blue sea
Blow the wind southerly, southerly, southerly
Blow bonnie breeze my lover to me.

Edward enters, the cold and rain coming with him. He's drenched. Helen shoots a look of reproach.

(*Softly.*) Where have you been?

Edward Walking. It's awfully wet.

Edward takes off his wet oilskin and shakes it out.

Helen (*indicates the baby*) Shh!

Helen only knows one verse of the song, so she sings it again:

Blow the wind southerly, southerly, southerly
Blow the wind south o'er the bonnie blue sea
Blow the wind southerly, southerly, southerly
Blow bonnie breeze my lover to me.

Helen is tired. Edward takes the baby from her: 'Let me.' Helen is grateful. She takes Edward's wet things and leaves the room. Edward rocks the baby and sings, in a bright, clear voice:

Edward

They told me last night there were ships in the offing
And I hurried down to the deep rolling sea
But I could not see it, wherever might be it
The bark that is bearing my true love to me.

As Edward sings, he takes a rusty service revolver from his jacket pocket. He stares at it.

He has the pistol in one hand and the baby in the other as Helen re-enters.

Helen Are you coming to bed?

Edward tries to stuff the revolver back in his pocket, but he fumbles, and it falls to the floor with a clatter. They both stare at it. Then Helen moves swiftly to take the baby.

Give me Myfanwy.

Edward hands the baby to Helen, hastily picks up his gun, and exits upstairs.

SCENE FOUR

1913. Robert Frost, thirty-nine, blond-haired, blue-eyed and handsome, leaves a London restaurant, buttoning up his overcoat.

Helen still has the baby in her arms.

Helen (*to us*) Their first meeting was at a vegetarian restaurant on St Martin's Lane, after some sort of literary luncheon. Edward used to go to town once a week, and come back with books to review. I don't know what took Robert there. It was the tail end of nineteen thirteen, and nothing was the same after nineteen thirteen, absolutely nothing at all.

Helen leaves. Edward runs out of the restaurant, a pile of new books under his arm, and approaches Robert.

Edward I say! Mr Frost! Hold on! – I'm Thomas, Edward Thomas.

Robert Oh, yeah, you're –

Edward I've reviewed you, yes.

Robert (*shaking hands*) It's a pleasure.

Edward Yes, for me too. Hello.

They stand awkwardly for a minute. Neither is well dressed.

It's a good place, isn't it, the St George's? Did you enjoy your lunch?

Robert Ah. Sure.

Edward You seem uncertain.

Robert (*laughs*) It's not a menu that – it's not what I normally have.

Edward What do you normally have?

Robert Well – not nut cutlets. Not bean stew. Steak, if I have any money.

Edward Have you got any money?

Robert No.

They laugh.

Edward My doctor says I must forgo meat. And alcohol. And coffee. And sugar. And excitement of all kinds.

Robert Not much to live for, then.

Edward Barely anything. Poetry, I suppose.

Robert (*laughing*) I guess. – You incline to poor health?

Edward I incline to misery. They think it's linked to my digestion – thus demonstrating the great advance of medicine since fifteen sixty-eight.

Robert My wife says I'm miserable, too.

Edward You don't look it.

Robert Americans aren't allowed to be depressed. We have it enshrined in the Constitution. But I married a woman who thought I was a god. Maybe a demi-god. Some species of genius, anyhow. I haven't quite lived up to the billing.

Edward You've written some first-rate verse.

Robert Thanks. Think anyone will buy it?

Edward Depends on the reviews.

Robert Well, yours have certainly helped.

Edward Good, I'm glad. I'll tell my wife someone thinks it's worth it.

Robert Is she, uh –?

Edward I also married a girl who believed I'd do great things. I see the disappointment in her eyes.

Robert I know that look. You got children?

Edward Three.

Robert I've four.

Edward Something else we have in common.

Robert I'm sure we've much. Just don't invite me for supper, OK?

Edward I haven't two ha'pennies to rub together, or I'd invite you to –

He staggers, feeling faint.

Robert What is it? Thomas?

Edward I'm all right. Just dizzy –

Robert What's the matter?

Edward It's just London . . . My head thumps, I've a belly-ache, I don't sleep a wink . . . I hate London! Thank God I no longer live here.

Robert Where do you live?

Edward In Hampshire. You?

Robert We've been in Beaconsfield, in a sort of box, what do you call it? – a 'bungalow'. We're getting out, going down to Gloucestershire for a year. Gibson and Abercrombie – you know them? – they've found us an old cottage.

Edward I know them well. They're good poets. Well, good-ish.

Robert Forgive me, I'm a stranger – but are you a poet yourself?

Edward Me? No. I couldn't write a poem to save my life! – I'm fine, now, thanks, Frost. I'm heading for Waterloo, how about you?

Robert Marylebone.

Edward I don't mind walking that way. Who have you been reading? Anything good?

They head off, talking together.

SCENE FIVE

1914. Night. A harvest moon. Helen Thomas in her overcoat and hat. She isn't fashionably dressed – indeed, she's poor – and her taste in clothes tends to a kind of early hippy look. She puts down two suitcases.

Helen (*to us*) On the fifth of August, nineteen fourteen, we set out to visit the Frosts. Edward and Merfyn had cycled ahead and found us some rooms in a farmhouse, so I had Bronwen, the baby and the Russian boy from Bedales. And the bloody dog. We left from Petersfield on what should have been a simple journey, through Oxford to Gloucester, change for Ledbury. But of course they had just declared war, so imagine the commotion! There were families rushing home from their holidays, reservists called up, trunks and kitbags and cancellations and delays, and we started and stopped and started and stopped until long after midnight we reached Malvern, where the stationmaster wouldn't let us sleep on the platform, and I've three little children and a dog! Finally a taxi we could scarce afford brought us out to Dymock. I shall never forget driving through the Malvern Hills, under a harvest moon, on the very first night of the war. (*She's exhausted.*) Coo-ee! Edward?

Edward (*off*) Coo-ee!

Helen Coo-ee!

Edward enters at a run.

Edward Helen! Thank God.

They embrace, a little stiffly.

Helen In future, remind me not to start my holiday the day the Kaiser invades Belgium.

Edward Was it an awful journey?

Helen Yes. A policeman stopped the car in Ledbury, wanting to know our names. When Yuri said he was Russian, the poor man wet himself. He thought we were spies!

Edward Really?

Helen Yes!

They laugh.

Oh, I shouldn't laugh. We're at war! But oh.

Edward I know. But Helen, it's wonderful here. Perfect walking country. Look, across the meadow – can you see in the moonlight? – that's Little Iddens. The half-timbered house? That's where the Frosts are.

Helen Shall we be seeing much of them?

Edward Every day, I expect.

Helen Every day?

Edward Well, Frost and I go out every day.

Helen Oh, I see. You're fond of him, aren't you?

Edward We find we've much to discuss.

Helen But you genuinely like him, don't you?

Edward Aren't I allowed to like him?

Helen I wasn't *suggesting* anything!

Edward I've reviewed him, Helen. That's what I do.

Helen Three times. You've reviewed him three times. The same book.

Edward Well? It's a good book.

Helen Is it? I thought it a bit banal.

Edward Banal?

Helen I haven't finished it, I haven't had time, but – the language is just everyday speech. Is that really poetry?

Edward To what do we owe this sudden facility for literary criticism? Did you pick it up on the train?

He strides off into the farmhouse.

Helen (*to us*) That wasn't the real Edward. The real Edward's not moody and spiteful. The real Edward is kind and sweet, the shy boy I lay with on Wimbledon Common, what seems like a lifetime ago. But it's so easy to say the wrong thing. And then – oh! – the sulking. The silence. The children bored in rented rooms. That August was bloody hard work.

Helen picks up the suitcases and follows him in.

SCENE SIX

Warmth and dappled sunlight, a glorious summer's day. Edward enters with Robert. They wear their walking clothes: collars, ties, waistcoats, knapsacks – though as a concession to the hot weather they are carrying their jackets. They hugely enjoy each other's company.

Robert And then it's over?

Edward No, then it's *an* over. Six balls make an over. Unless there's a bye.

Robert Someone leaves the field?

He waves 'goodbye'.

Edward (*laughing*) No! Someone might leave the field, but then the twelfth man would come on.

Robert I thought you said there were eleven.

Edward There are eleven. But always a twelfth.

Robert Who's that? The Other Man? (*He grins.*) And this little jar with the ashes of the sticks, the stumps, this is the greatest prize in cricket?

Edward There is no greater.

Robert I've got to say, we do things differently in New Hampshire.

Laughing, they come to a stile, and rest. Robert picks up a stick and toys with it. Eventually, he snaps it in two.

Edward Well, I live in Old Hampshire, and that's how we do things there. It's just an excuse to stand in a field, smell the turf, watch a row of swaying poplars by the boundary . . . a lazy heron passing deep extra cover . . .

Robert A whole new approach to competitive sport.

Pause.

I like this country.

Edward Stay.

Robert Small matter of a war you're about to have. – Don't you smoke cigarettes?

Edward has taken out a long-stemmed clay pipe, and now packs it with York River tobacco, and eventually lights it.

Edward I gave up smoking. Doctor's orders.

Robert Oh, this isn't smoking?

Edward Not really. This is keeping alive a fast disappearing rural tradition. The main difficulty is in getting the thing to ignite. You need a denser pack than with a briar; but my opinion is that if a chap can manage to light it, he ought to be allowed to smoke it.

Robert To keep alive a rural tradition.

Edward Exactly. And the beauty of a clay is it can be cured, d'you see? If a pipe gets a taint, lay it on the hot coals, right in the heart of the fire. It either comes out broken or perfect.

Robert recoils from the fug which issues from Edward's pipe.

Robert How does Helen feel about this?

Edward Same way she feels about everything.

Robert . . . You and she don't rub along so well.

Edward Helen could be the happiest woman on earth, if I'd only let her. But I can't. I get low, damned low, and then I'm rotten company, and then I hate myself. One day I climbed Shoulder-of-Mutton Hill with a revolver in my pocket. But I couldn't see it through. I went back for my tea, as always.

Robert I set out once for the Dismal Swamp with no intention to return.

Edward The Dismal Swamp? Where's that?

Robert In North Carolina.

Edward What's it like?

Robert Wet, with alligators.

Edward Alligators? Gosh. What happened?

Robert Well, see, I hung around just long enough to feel extremely foolish. Then I went home for my tea.

Edward The curse of indecision.

Robert No. I have made my decisions. My wife, she's not robust. There are four kids to feed, and – I have to pitch in, that's all there is to it. I can't go killing myself, I got to scrape potatoes.

Edward Good Lord, I don't do any of that. Cooking and cleaning. You do that?

Robert Yep. No harm in it.

Edward I just don't have the time. Besides, I need to get away to work. I go away for months at a stretch.

Robert Where do you go?

Edward Cumberland. Norfolk. All over.

Robert But don't you feel your duty lies at home?

Edward Home? Home is just a place you dry your boots.

Robert You really mean that?

Edward I don't feel I really belong anywhere, d'you see? I love my family, but living with them . . . in the same house as them . . . it's insufferable. How's a man supposed to concentrate? The din! The baby! The hysteria! And we're in such straits, from one month to the next, what with the school fees and the – the – I feel so inadequate. I'm quite useless! I think the only thing is divorce.

He sees a wild flower.

I say, here's something. Well, how-do-you-do?

He is bending to look.

Robert What is it?

Edward I thought you went to Harvard?

Robert Yeah, but your plants are different than ours.

Edward This is purple-headed wood betony. Very popular in the Middle Ages.

Robert Looks like Ezra Pound in his Oriental dressing gown.

Edward He's a colourful fellow.

Robert He's an incredible ass.

Edward He gave you a decent review.

Robert He said I was 'a little raw' – like I was some kind of ruralist! He said, 'This man has the good sense to speak naturally' – as if the poems came out by accident. By fluke!

Edward Still, Ezra liked them, as did I.

Robert But you liked them because you understood them! What he saw in them isn't there and what is there he couldn't have seen or he wouldn't have liked them! And now he has the hide to tell me I oughta be writing free verse! Free verse? I'd as soon play tennis with the net down! – Don't leave Helen. She loves you, you know.

Edward Perhaps, but she expects nothing back.

Robert She doesn't?

Edward No.

Robert Why not?

Edward I've told her not to expect it.

Robert I bet that cleared the air in the kitchen.

Edward Look, her life has been . . . Her mother is a hard woman. They fell out over, well, me. Helen ran off to Broadstairs and worked as a governess. She has a low opinion of her abilities, and no expectation of pleasure. One wouldn't want to confuse her by being too nice.

He lapses into silence and fiddles with his pipe.

Robert Ed, I didn't mean to upset you. I thought we were buddies.

Edward Then we are.

Robert Then nothing should remain unsaid between us.

Edward Then nothing shall.

Robert Can I ask a real hard question?

Edward You may.

Robert How do we get back from here? I'm lost!

Edward (*happily*) Let's have a look!

He pulls out his map and spreads it on the ground.

We can either cross the Leadon at Ketford – go over Monk's Bridge, and up through Tiller's Green to Leddington; or, we could strike north through Ryton Coppice, and call on Abercrombie at The Gallows.

Robert Well, which is best?

Edward Hard to say. It would be nice to see Abercrombie, but he might be out. However there's always the Gibsons. They'll give us a cup of tea there.

Robert Fine, let's do that.

Edward But if we skirt Dymock to the north, we'll lose the view of May Hill at dusk.

Robert Worth seeing?

Edward Certainly.

Robert Then let's go that way.

Edward It'd be a shame to miss Abercrombie.

Robert Then let's go the other way.

Edward Though he might be out.

Robert So we'll see the Gibsons instead.

Edward Oh, it's impossible! That road or this? – What's funny?

Robert is gently laughing at him. Bott, a gamekeeper, enters. A fat and ruddy countryman with a shotgun broken open in the crook of his arm.

Bott What are you jack-the-lads up to? This is Lord Beauchamp's land!

Edward Yes, we know that, we're –

Bott Lord Beauchamp's land! So get your shabby arse off it! And you, lad!

Robert Hey, fella, just a minute –

Bott Damned cottagers! What you trying for, then? His Lordship's game, is it?

Edward We're not poaching, we're –

Bott Oh arr?

Edward Look, I'm ever so sorry, we've been given permission to –

Robert (*angrily*) We're just taking a walk, OK? Is this country still feudal or –

Bott You're foreign. You a German?

Robert I'm an American.

Bott American? You a spy?

Robert No, gee, I am not a spy!

Bott They'm saying there's spies all over Dymock! Russians, Christ knows what! Get off this land 'fore I shoots you! Get!

Edward We're going! – Come on.

Edward backs away, and so does Robert, but then Robert suddenly changes his mind and advances on Bott. His anger is greater than his fear.

Robert See here, fellow, I don't allow people to speak to me that way! We have permission to be in these woods, and you can either make your apologies, or you can put up your fists!

He shapes up for a fight.

I'm not a poacher, I am a true-blood Yankee farmer, and you are a fat British bastard!

Edward shelters timidly behind Robert.

Bott I'll bag the pair o' you for the pot!

Bott advances towards Robert, locks his shotgun barrel, brings it up to his eye, and sights. Robert skips out of the way. Bott bears down on Edward. Edward tries to hide, genuinely very frightened.

Edward Don't shoot! Please don't shoot!

Edward cowers on the ground.

Bott You piss yourself, boy?

Robert Ed! Stand up!

Edward runs off. Bott swivels and aims at Robert. He cocks the hammer. Robert raises his hands.

OK. I'm not quarrelling with that.

Bott Get off His Lordship's land.

SCENE SEVEN

Outside the Thomases' lodgings. Helen's statuesque figure is tanned from long hours working outside.

Helen (*to us*) When I was young I used to love my body. I loved being without clothes, moving about naked. I took pride in my health and strength.

Edward enters and sits on a stool, staring morosely at the floor. Helen busies herself with household chores.

(*To Edward.*) The keeper was just doing his job! You have nothing to chide yourself with!

Edward You've no idea what you're talking about.

Helen Yes I have, you were sensible enough to –

Edward I ran away. Whereas Frost –

Helen Oh, Frost this, Frost that, Frost is just another amateur, you know, like Abercrombie and the rest! Not one of them has an eighth of your talent! Don't you know how highly they regard you?

Edward Helen, they think I'm a failed writer, who now makes his living as a critic.

Helen That's absolute rot. You've written more in the last three months than they'll ever manage in a lifetime.

Edward Oh, Helen –

Helen No, they're wonderful books!

Edward Wonderful books? Biography of Marlborough, seventy-five thousand words in twenty-six days? *Flowers of the British Isles* – all of 'em – in three weeks flat? Twenty sides a day no matter what, and everything written to order? I'm a hack, that's all there is to it. Frost is a poet.

Helen He's forty and only just published!

Edward Well, it was worth the wait. Do you know what his work actually does? Have you any idea?

Helen Er –

Edward It asks the question: 'What is poetry?'

Helen All right. Good. What's the answer?

Edward Don't you see? It's entirely original, it will change the face of modern verse! (*Bitterly.*) Set that against the Duke of Marlborough.

Helen But Edwy, I love you, the children love you, we're proud of you, we know how hard you work for us, how much you've had to compromise –

Edward I'm sick of everything. Sick of you, sick of the children, whom I know really despise me, although they couldn't despise me as much as I despise myself for not putting an end to the wretched business! – Stop that! I don't want you fussing around me. I know what I am, I know what I've done to you. Go away.

Helen I am so sorry you are blue. I had high hopes for this holiday, I really thought you'd enjoy it.

Edward I am enjoying it, who said I wasn't?

Helen Well, from what you've –

Edward I'm having a splendid time. I'm never so well as when going twenty or thirty miles with Frost. Never so well at all!

Helen Then why are you so beastly when you come home to me?

Edward takes out his clay pipe.

Must you light that thing?

Edward immediately stands up and strides off.

Edward! It's nearly teatime! Where are –

But Edward exits.

(*To us.*) Rob Frost became famous very shortly after, his reputation built on those early reviews of my husband's. He went back to Boston and – oh, such fame! They've named a mountain after him. It's in Vermont. They haven't named much after Edward. There's a plaque on a rock on Shoulder-of-Mutton Hill, but – Christ, but – oh, I can't get bitter about it, jealousy's not in my nature, it's all water under the bridge. All past! But that August was bloody hard work.

Eleanor (*off*) Coo-ee!

Helen Until Eleanor arrived.

Eleanor (*off*) Hello!

Helen We always cheered up mightily when Eleanor arrived.

Edward enters with Eleanor Farjeon, thirty-three. Eleanor is short and a bit round, shy, giggly, wearing rimless glasses, a summery dress and a floppy hat. She staggers under the weight of a massive haversack. She is socially a cut above the Thomases. Edward is happy.

Edward Look who's here!

Helen Eleanor, darling –

Eleanor Hello! I found you!

Helen Welcome to Dymock.

Edward *Now* we shall have fun.

Eleanor Helen, you look brown.

Helen The weather's been tremendous.

Edward What about me? Do I look brown?

Eleanor Who would know? You're dressed for November! Who knows if you're brown or not?

Edward laughs and helps Eleanor to wriggle out of her pack.

Edward What have you got in here?

Eleanor Presents!

Helen Oh, Eleanor – you shouldn't –

Eleanor Just a few things for the children. I know times are hard. And with this coming war –

Edward No! No talk of war today. – I'll drop this over to the farmhouse, see if your rooms are ready. Back in a jiffy!

He takes up her haversack and exits.

Eleanor I walked up through the orchards. All the pears and plums! – Greengages, nectarines! – Rich, rich soil. What a gorgeous part of England! (*Lowers her voice.*) How is he?

Helen He thinks he's got – what is it? – neurasthenia.

Eleanor Oh, dear!

Helen (*sighs*) Yes. It'll mean another idiotic diet.

Eleanor tentatively hugs Helen.

Eleanor Everything will be all right.

Helen I thought this trip might refresh him. Thought we might start again. But he's only content when he's with Robert Frost, wittering on about words.

Eleanor Words?

Helen Words, words, the meaning of words! As if it wasn't obvious!

Eleanor I am curious to meet Mr Frost. What's he like?

Helen Well, he's American. (*Whispers.*) The children don't have a bedtime. They go to sleep when they want!

Eleanor raises an eyebrow in disbelief.

SCENE EIGHT

A barn. Stooks of hay. Robert and Edward return from a long day's walking. Robert is in full flow, fiddling with a stick as he talks.

Robert The living part of a poem is the intonation entangled in the syntax, idiom and meaning of a sentence. But what *is* a sentence? OK, I'll give you a new definition. A sentence is a *sound* in itself on which other sounds called words may be strung – like laundry on a line. Here's the line – here's the laundry – see? – all that irregularity of accent across the regular beat of the metre. These sentence-sounds are very definite, they are as definite as words. They are gathered by the ear from the vernacular and brought on to the page. I think no writer invents them, the most original writer only catches them fresh from talk. Words exist in the mouth, not in books, and you can't read a single good sentence with the salt in it unless you have previously heard it spoken. That's what I think. The ear does it all, the ear is the only true writer and the only true reader. And this sentence-sound often says more than the words. It may even – as in irony – convey a meaning opposite to the words. So to judge a poem you apply the one test, the big test. You listen for the sentence-sounds. If you find some of those – caught fresh from the mouths of people – and definite and recognizable and true – you know you have found a writer. War on cliché!

Edward War on rhetoric!

Robert War on free verse!

They laugh cheerfully. Robert snaps the stick he is holding, and throws away the pieces.

Edward Why do you do that?

Robert Huh?

Edward *That?*

Robert I like the sound. There was a brook running through my property . . . we called it Hyla Brook . . . I'd go sit there and snap sticks. You ever – ?

Edward I've never had any property.

Robert None?

Edward My father came up to London to sit the Civil Service Exam. For this he had to teach himself French, Latin and German. He then became a clerk in the department of rail and tram traffic at the Board of Trade. And there he remains. No, I've never had any land.

Helen and Eleanor enter. They have flagons of cider and five pewter mugs, and a sewing basket. It's a warm evening. Helen's arms are bare, her hair is down, she has bare feet and no underskirts.

Helen Hello!

Robert Hey, Helen.

Helen Where did you go today?

Robert Up on May Hill. Boy!

Edward You have the Severn and the Cotswolds on one hand, and on the other the Wye, the Forest of Dean, and beyond the Black Mountains of Wales!

Robert And he showed me every contour on his map.

Laughter. Helen pours drinks.

Helen Rob, we have cider and perry – will Mrs Frost come down?

Robert She's not been well – the heat – I doubt that –

Edward Eleanor, let me introduce you – this is Miss Farjeon. Robert Frost.

Eleanor (*shaking hands*) How do you do?

Robert I'm pretty fine, Miss Farjeon.

Edward Eleanor's here for the rest of August.

Helen Cider or perry?

Edward Cider. The children?

Helen They're already in bed. (*To Robert.*) I wouldn't know about yours.

Robert I'll go in soon. I'm beat. (*To Eleanor.*) I've been today on a botanising walk – miles and miles we went! – but I've seen more species than I ever knew existed!

Eleanor Oh, I'm hopeless with plants. Bronwen's been trying to teach me their names – mouse-eared hawkweed, birdfoot trefoil – but I've a memory like a sieve and although I worship the country I'm not an expert like Edward or a farmer like yourself.

Robert Well, I call myself a farmer, but I couldn't keep the cow in milk. Couldn't keep the weeds from the bean rows. Couldn't get the hens to lay – that was particularly embarrassing.

Helen Why?

Robert It was a poultry farm. In the end we had to sell.

Eleanor What brought you here, Mr Frost?

Robert A powerful desire to mix with men of letters. I had gotten it into my head I was a poet. I had to come here to achieve it.

Eleanor And have you enjoyed your time in England?

Robert Lady, I've published two books of poems!

Laughter and cheers.

And my family have lived under thatch, and seen the King, and ate lardy-cake, and heard for the first time a skylark, a cuckoo, your English blackbird – a romance such as happens to few – and I've met Yeats, and Edward here, and Monro at the Poetry Bookshop –

Edward Eleanor's also a writer.

Robert That so? What do you write, Miss Farjeon?

Eleanor Oh, it's all troubadours and minstrels and – you wouldn't like it – aubades and serenades and –

Edward She wrote an opera when she was eighteen.

Helen Did you?

Eleanor With my brother, yes.

Helen Good Lord. When I was eighteen I was –

Edward How is Bertie?

Helen – in Broadstairs.

Eleanor He's thinking of enlisting.

It's getting dark outside. Helen lights the storm lanterns, sits down by one and threads her darning needle. Edward lights his clay pipe. Helen doesn't object. They all sit with their drinks, peacefully. The sounds of evening drift in.

Robert He doesn't have to, does he? Enlist?

Eleanor No. But they can't invade Belgium willy-nilly. Someone has to teach them a lesson. At least that's what Bertie says.

Robert He's right.

Helen He is not right. Sorry.

Robert (*laughing, but displeased*) Your wife has opinions, Ed.

Helen At Bedales we don't believe anything will be solved by embarking on another ghastly war.

Robert Bedales?

Helen It's the school in our village, it's where Bronwen and Merfyn go, I teach there sometimes – not formally, I'm not qualified, but I get invited to lots of meetings and picnics and debates.

Edward It's 'progressive'. They take girls.

Helen They take pacifism awfully seriously, and I think they're right.

Edward They take sandals awfully seriously, and their feet get wet.

Helen But what is it going to accomplish? A lot of young chaps will get killed, and for what?

Edward It's the defence of a principle.

Helen Oh, balls!

Edward Helen!

Helen I shouldn't curse but oh! The only reason we're fighting is that unemployment has got out of hand.

Eleanor I don't think Bertie –

Helen No, Bertie isn't unemployed, I don't suppose lots in Hampstead are, but –

Edward But many young men are proud to do their – Why, even Merfyn is saying –

Helen (*darning*) My son is never going to fight in an imperialist war, and that's that.

Edward He may feel he has a duty to –

Helen You never talk to him, how would you know?

Edward We cycled here from Petersfield!

Helen Yes, but did you *talk* to him? Did you? Anyway, he's too young for politics.

Edward There are things more important than politics, as you know perfectly well!

Helen Such as?

Edward Good grief, Helen, really anything's more important than politics! Birdsong's more important than politics!

Helen laughs. He digs in.

The birds – I am perfectly serious – the birds may know secrets that we don't.

Helen War is idiotic. There must be a better way to settle arguments. If the bloody blue-tits know what it is, perhaps they'd like to tell us.

Edward is quietly fuming.

Eleanor (*to Robert*) May I ask about *North of Boston*? How did you light on that style? It is awfully distinctive – revolutionary, Edward says.

Robert I had some character strokes I had to get in somewhere, and I chose a sort of eclogue form for them, that's all.

Eleanor I'm not sure what –

Robert OK, it's a dialogue on pastoral themes: Virgil's *Bucolica*, Spenser's *Shepherd's Calendar* – they're eclogues. I dropped into that form, but I used an everyday level of diction, a level of diction that even Wordsworth kept above. A language absolutely un-literary – just the voices of farming people in New Hampshire where I live.

Eleanor And how do you hear these voices, if you're not farming people yourself?

Robert I pick up the telephone, and eavesdrop. (*He winks.*) That must be our little secret.

Helen You've a telephone? In your house?

Robert It was a party line, we shared it with several homesteads. (*To Eleanor.*) So when it rings I pick up the earpiece and I listen in, if it's for me or if it isn't! Keeping the kids quiet is the hard part.

Edward That sounds suspiciously like cheating.

Eleanor 'He cheated at poetry.' Now there's an epitaph.

Robert Oh, I got a better one, if we're talking headstones.

Edward We are.

Robert 'I had a lover's quarrel with the world.'

Edward is impressed.

But not so fast, Miss Farjeon. I'm not ready for burial yet – intend to stick around for a good while to come!

Laughter.

Eleanor I hope you do! But how do you define what forms of everyday language are appropriate for verse? There must be some constructions that simply don't work?

Robert I decided that I would use only words or combinations of words that I had *heard* in running speech. We've got to find a new grammar for poetry, not imagist, not symbolist, above all not modernist, but real, and true.

Helen Oh, Edward's been saying that for years.

Edward Helen, please!

Helen You have! In the Swinburne book! In the Pater! You're always banging on about colloquial speech! On and on and on!

Edward Well, I won't be banging on for much longer, will I? Who's going to want a monograph on Swinburne, now? Who's going to publish me at all? I don't know what to do.

Robert Come to America.

Helen America!

Edward He didn't mean you.

Eleanor takes around the jug of cider. She pours first for Helen. Helen is drinking hard.

Robert Maybe we could get another farm. Maybe not chickens. Fruit trees. Come and help me pick some fruit.

Edward Rob, I'm a writing animal, I doubt that I –

Robert But consider it, OK?

Edward Thanks.

Pause.

When are you going back?

Eleanor Would you like some more cider?

Robert Yes, please. (*To Edward.*) I don't know.

Eleanor Watch out, it's strong.

Eleanor takes the cider to Edward.

Would you like some?

Edward No. Yes. No, I've had enough. – Eleanor? I will. The truth is, I never know what I should do.

Robert You should write poetry, that's what you should do.

Edward I can't, you know I can't –

Eleanor Oh, you should!

Edward I've tried, but –

Robert Try again!

Edward It all comes out so –

Robert Because you're drowning in words! You're suffocating in biographies and monographs and godfrey knows what!

Edward We have to eat! So I have to write!

Robert But at this moment you're writing as good poetry as anyone alive, except it's in prose form! It doesn't *look* like a poem – yet it is! Let it declare itself as what it is, what it longs to be. Pick up your *In Pursuit of Spring* – the loveliest book on springtime anyone ever wrote – take some paragraphs – from any page! – and put them down in verse form, in exactly the same cadence. Make it a poem. It'll work!

Edward (*smiling*) Is poetry the most important thing in the world?

Robert Yes, of course!

Edward Why?

Robert Because it offers us a momentary stay against confusion. Some chance of order in the chaos.

Edward Sounds good.

Robert Doesn't it?

Edward Does it work?

Eleanor Oh, do try! You must! You must!

Edward (*to Eleanor, ruefully*) Did anyone ever begin at thirty-six in the shade?

Robert Are you afeared? – Is he afeared?

Eleanor Edward isn't afraid of anything.

Helen He's afraid of my mother.

Laughter.

Edward I'm afraid of failure. I confess I am afraid of that.

Eleanor Oh, don't be such a silly! – Sing something. I love to hear you sing.

Edward sings some verses of a mournful Welsh folk song. For some moments they are all lost in their thoughts. Edward finishes, and there is a pause.

Robert What was that? Welsh?

Edward Yes.

Helen God, they're gloomy.

Edward My people aren't gloomy. They're –

Helen I've got one.

Helen stands, determined to liven up the party, and sings 'I know where I'm going'. She takes it at a brisk pace.

I know where I'm going
And who's going with me

I know who I love
But the devil knows who I'll marry.

Edward and Eleanor laugh with recognition and join in. Robert claps along to the beat.

Helen, Edward *and* **Eleanor**
I'll have stockings of silk
Shoes of bright green leather
Combs to buckle my hair
And a ring for every finger.

Helen dances, increasingly wildly. She kicks up her skirts, showing her bare legs, singing faster and faster. Eleanor looks plump and mousey beside her, which is probably the intention.

Helen, Edward *and* **Eleanor**
Featherbeds are soft
Painted rooms are bonny
I would leave them all
Just to be with my love Johnny.

Some say that he's poor
But I say that he's bonny
Fairest of them all
My handsome winsome Johnny.

Robert watches Helen's display with a mixture of disgust and fascination.

Helen, Edward and Eleanor keep laughing and singing, faster and faster. Helen falls into Edward's arms and kisses him. Eleanor watches with a smile. Then she slips away and exits.

Edward pours more cider and begins to sing a love song:

Edward
As I walked out one May morning
So early in the spring

I placed my back against the old garden gate
And I heard my true love sing.

To hear my true love sing, my boys
To hear what she had for to say
'Tis now very near three-quarters of a year
Since you and I together did lay.

Come now my love and sit down by me
Where the leaves are springing green
'Tis now very near three-quarters of a year
Since you and I together have been.

Helen (*to us*) By the time we next had a holiday, Robert was back in America, and Edward was dead.

Robert drains his cider, smiling at Edward with affection, as Edward concludes the song:

Edward
I will not come and sit down by you
Nor yet nor other young man
Since you've been courting some other young girl
Your heart is no longer mine.

Robert leaves, waving.

Robert Goodnight!

Helen *and* **Edward** 'Night, Rob! 'Night!

Helen turns down the lanterns. Edward finishes his drink.

Helen (*tired*) Shall we go to bed?

Edward takes hold of Helen in the dark.

Edward Helen?

Helen Yes, love?

Edward I'm sorry.

Edward exits.

Helen (*to us*) In nineteen fifty-seven, Rob returned to England. Goodness, hadn't we aged! By nineteen fifty-seven he was feted as the poet of the people, the salt of the earth, the bard of small-town America. He was to receive honorary degrees from Oxford and Cambridge, and we were all in a state of high excitement. Robert Frost was coming to tea! Eleanor organised transport, and Myfanwy and I made the food. We'd seen him briefly at a reception, where he had important people to meet, but he was coming to us! He was coming! Eleanor went to collect him in the car. But when she got to the Embassy they said he had a sore throat, he wasn't coming, he couldn't go. A sore throat? He didn't have a sore throat when he was chatting with T. S. Eliot! He didn't have a sore throat when Auden wanted a word! And Bronwen was there, and Merfyn, and we had salmon and mayonnaise, and watercress, and the wine chilling in the chalk stream. But no Robert.

I heard that he went down to Dymock. Sat by Little Iddens, and wept. Then he went home with his caps and his gowns, and I never saw him again.

SCENE NINE

Edward enters, leaning into the wind. It's raining hard. He wears his hat and oilskin, and carries a stout stick. He is trying to catch up with someone.

Edward Hey! You!

There's someone away off in the distance, but we can't see.

Yes! You! Stop! Who are you?

Edward waves his hat.

Hey! Wait! – Wherever I go, you are there before me! Whenever I rest, you rest! Who are you? Why do you seem so familiar? (*With fear and wonder.*) Are you the Other Man?

Edward goes off after the stranger.

SCENE TEN

Hampstead. Eleanor works in her study.

Eleanor (*to us*) And then very suddenly he started writing poems. December, nineteen fourteen.

Edward enters, and shrugs off his knapsack.

He sent them straight to Hampstead – would I type them out? I felt blessed. He'd asked *me*!

Edward takes manuscripts from his bag.

Edward I've more.

Eleanor Gracious!

Edward I am in it and no mistake!

They laugh happily.

Eleanor (*to us*) Suddenly he was undammed! A hundred and forty-three poems in two years! What's the machinery, what's the spring? How does a poet become a poet?

Edward Every day I run to my study. I have a sort of glimpse of perfection, I can't wait to get to work!

Eleanor Why, what has happened, Edward?

Edward I couldn't say! I did what Frost told me to. Took a few lines of prose – and – look! (*He takes up a page.*) D'you see? This one was called 'Old Man's Beard' at first. But I think 'Old Man' is better because –

Eleanor It's Lad's-Love, isn't it?

Edward Yes. Or Maiden's-Ruin.

Eleanor (*laughs*) Yes.

Edward So I took some lines from my notebook and –

Eleanor (*reading*) Is that Myfanwy picking the herb?

Edward Yes, it grows by the kitchen door.

Eleanor The little angel. I love your children! – May I show these to Bertie?

Edward No, don't show them to anybody.

Eleanor But Helen's read them?

He nods.

What does she think?

Edward She thinks they're as good as Frost's. But they're not. His are – Eleanor, d'you see? – his poems are masterpieces, of deep and mysterious tenderness. I'm just an apprentice, a chick in the nest, working up some field notes into verse.

Eleanor But Helen –

Edward Helen rarely knows whereof she speaks.

Eleanor She might in this instance be right.

Edward No, she's not right.

Eleanor Well, I'm tempted to agree with her.

Edward No, you're not tempted to agree with her, you're just tempted to take her side.

Eleanor Why would I do that?

Edward Because you like her!

Eleanor Of course I like her! Don't you?

Edward I'm married to her, it's not the same.

Eleanor Surely you liked her when you married her?

Edward I had far rather talk about poetry. Frost has a theory that –

Eleanor Your poetry is threaded through with love.

Edward No it isn't.

Eleanor Oh, but it is!

Edward I don't love. I can't.

Eleanor Tush, you must! Even if –

Edward I don't.

Eleanor (*teasing*) You do! You do!

Edward I'm not capable of it! I don't!

Eleanor Edward Thomas! You do!

Edward (*laughing, finally*) All right! I do.

Eleanor Tell me what you love. Tell me.

Edward I love roads. Signposts. Sheep tracks over the Downs. The wind, the rain. The mud. I love mud!

Pause.

What do you love, Eleanor?

Eleanor I love your writing. Your prose is good, it's very good, but – these poems! They are audacious, they are marvellous, Edward, they are marvellous. I think to myself – what is he going to do next?

Edward I'm going to give up trying to be clever. I'm going to throw away the last rags of rhetoric and formality which have left my prose dead on the page, long lines of words laid out on the page, a great graveyard of letters. When I get it right I feel I touch something ancient and true. The stab of memory, the ache of loss. I say, do you know what I'm getting at?

Eleanor Yes, I do – as if we're missing something we never quite knew that we had.

Edward Yes, because the old myths are being destroyed –

Eleanor Yes, trampled underfoot –

Edward The old country ways are nearly gone. But there is a world, Eleanor, there's a place inaccessible to stupidity, greed, progress –

Eleanor Oh, Edward –

Edward – the world of imagination.

Eleanor Oh yes. Man is at war with nature.

Edward No, I don't oppose nature to man. Quite the contrary. Man seems to me a very little part of nature, and the part I enjoy least.

Eleanor You must publish these.

Edward Under a pseudonym, perhaps. If anyone will take them.

Eleanor Why not your own name?

Edward What do you think they'd say if they knew it was me?

Eleanor Who?

Edward All the poor fellows I've reviewed in the past?

Eleanor They'll be impressed. As I am.

Edward You're too kind, I appreciate it.

Eleanor I'm not being kind.

Eleanor is gazing doe-eyed at him. Edward breaks away.

Edward Frost is decided. He's leaving. He's worried there may be a U-boat blockade. He wants to get his family out. Merfyn's going with him.

Eleanor Oh? Why?

Edward Merfyn is a great disappointment. He likes engineering. A spell in New England may buck up his ideas. How is Bertie enjoying the Army?

Eleanor He isn't in the Army any more.

Edward He isn't? It's only been a few weeks –

Eleanor He was invalided out. Varicose veins. He's getting married instead.

Edward Varicose veins? The medical sounds rather tough.

Eleanor Are you going to America too?

Edward Yes.

Eleanor When?

Edward Soon. In the summer. Maybe autumn. Well, soon.

Eleanor It's certain?

He hesitates.

Can't you make up your mind, dear?

Edward I can see a thousand reasons for going and a thousand reasons for staying. So I dither. Do I sound selfish?

Eleanor You sound Danish, frankly.

Edward (*laughs*) What, *Hamlet*? Every man thinks that was written for him. But I *know* it was written for me.

Eleanor (*laughs*) 'Hamlet, Prince of Petersfield'?

Edward (*laughs*) Yes. Think they'll get the joke in America?

Eleanor They'll adore you in America. But what about Helen?

Edward What about her?

Edward is suddenly morose.

Eleanor You wouldn't leave her behind? She does love you, Edward.

Edward Good Lord, I know *that*.

Eleanor You really ought to love her back.

Edward So they tell me.

And he's up and putting on his knapsack. Eleanor fetches a present, wrapped in fine paper, with a fancy bow.

What's this?

Eleanor Something I spotted on Jermyn Street.

Edward What is it?

Eleanor Open it and see.

Edward opens the parcel. It's a beautiful silk scarf.

Edward Oh, Eleanor –

Eleanor It's to keep you warm when you're out in the wind and rain.

Edward It's splendid! Thanks ever so much.

Eleanor Here –

Eleanor ties the scarf around his neck. She stands close, but there's no contact.

Now you look like a poet!

SCENE ELEVEN

Edward and Robert walk in the country. It's winter. Edward wears his scarf.

Robert I've put in an offer. It has a sugar-shack for maple syrup, and a good barn for the cow. Stands of birch, spruce, tamarack. An upper pasture and a hayfield.

Edward Tell me where it is again?

Robert Way up in New Hampshire. Views from the porch of Franconia Notch and Mount Lafayette. We'll walk the Northern Presidentials!

Edward Which are – ?

Robert Mountains, buddy. Real ones. Not like those bumps in the Malverns.

Edward You're ever so competitive, Robert.

Robert First principle of poetry. Knock the other guy down.

Edward I don't think I can operate like that.

Robert Sure you can. Come to Franconia. We'll farm and we'll write.

Edward But what'll I do for income?

Robert You'll get some lecturing, some readings, a stipend maybe – there's a market for guys like us! There are dollars to be made! But you got to be warm and approachable. You got to talk to fellows.

Edward I am warm and approachable.

Robert Ed, you're –

Edward What?

Robert It's OK.

Edward What?

Robert . . . I'd say you bristle easy.

Edward Nonsense. I go out of my way to be jolly. And when I'm blue, I go off on my own. Who could object to that? – I would certainly like to see those mountains.

Robert The Northern Presidentials! Mighty fine in the snow! Come on, come out to America – the greatest country that ever existed.

Edward It's not quite so simple, Rob. I've been commissioned to write an article – I had to take some work – on popular attitudes to the war. So I've been riding round, gathering material. And as I'm cycling I look at this country, which I love, and I realise that it's not genuinely mine unless I'm ready to protect it. I find myself asking, what does it mean to be English? To be part of this landscape, to have roots in the soil? What does it actually mean?

Robert What are you talking about? Who is more English than you?

Edward I want to come to Franconia. Genuinely I do. But I'm looking for something and I can't find it. And there must be a key! So I go about the world with a worried heart and a notebook, recording the weathercocks, the churches, the travellers' tales – trying to unlock who I am, where I'm from, what I'm for. There must be some good I can do! I've been useless for ever so long.

Robert A poet should prefer doing something well to doing good. There's plenty of saints. There ain't so many poets!

Robert marches off crossly. Edward waits, then follows.

SCENE TWELVE

Eleanor in her study, with sheaves of poems.

Eleanor (*to us*) He doesn't look back to a golden age, he looks at time itself. He speaks of things which may only be brushed with the fingertips . . . things liminal and loose, not to be held in the hand . . . struggles for survival, hard winters on hard earth. History. Memory. Something in the blood. And always walking west out of the city, in the tradition of the great dissenting walkers of old, the pounders of pavements, the prophets. And hearing the thrushes, the curlews, pewits, and crows – he believed that if we could translate their language, there's much to be learnt from the birds. And who's to say he's wrong? Edward knew the trees of every county. He would greet wild flowers as friends. He says we're inside nature, not outside, and nature's the only order, and it's harsh and accidental and always ends in death, and always begins with renewal. Unlike Frost he sees no higher power, no all-seeing eye, no man alone with his maker, hunched in the teeth of the storm. No salvation. No redemption. No God. Just the way things are and always were – the green shoots of spring, the birds' return from Africa, ale and songs at harvest-home – some pleasure in the here and now – or some half-remembered, wispy dream of pleasure, clutched at in between the squalls of rain.

SCENE THIRTEEN

The Thomases' cottage at Petersfield. Robert is waiting. Helen enters, her work-clothes muddy from the garden. She wears trousers. February 1915.

Helen Good morning.

Robert Good morning.

Helen Excuse the state of me, I've been digging. Now that the young chaps have all gone to France, the Bedales people say we must pitch in and help the village women in their gardens. We're going to grow all our veg together, and own it in common.

Robert Socialism comes to Petersfield?

Helen It's not really that kind of place.

Robert Thank the Lord for that.

Helen You disagree with socialism?

Robert I disagree with isms of all kinds. Don't like 'em, don't trust 'em, don't use 'em.

Helen What about pacifism? Humanism?

Robert I'd rather be a lone striker, Helen. I don't need to join a gang.

Helen You are going to look after my boy, aren't you?

Robert We're sailing in convoy, with a Royal Navy escort. Mrs Frost'll take good care of Merfyn.

Helen And do you think America will suit him?

Robert Well, I don't think it will suit him any worse than this Bedales crap, if you'll pardon my French.

Helen Robert! – I didn't know you spoke French.

Robert I don't.

Helen Oh, you should learn. It's taken usually as a mark of civilisation.

Robert Sorry, I forgot how civilised it is, these days, France.

Edward is approaching.

Edward (*off*) Hello! Rob?

Helen I don't know what I've done to so annoy you.

Robert (*softly*) Lady, men are dying in the trenches over there. The least that you could do is show support.

Edward enters.

Edward So you've come for Merfyn!

Robert We leave from Liverpool Tuesday. I'm saying my goodbyes.

Helen Well, goodbye.

She extends her muddy hand. Robert shakes it.

Robert Goodbye, Helen.

Helen I'll fetch Merfyn. (*To Edward.*) I hope you know what you're doing.

Helen leaves briskly. Robert wipes mud off his hand.

Edward What's got into her?

Robert I don't know, but maybe you should keep her tethered? Case she bites someone?

Edward (*laughs*) She's a free spirit, Rob, you can't tie her down.

Robert A free spirit?

Edward An elemental force.

Robert You trying to say you married a witch?

Edward No, I married a pretty girl from Wandsworth and set about destroying her, in which I seem to have not quite succeeded.

Robert The self-contempt, you know, it gets kind of tiresome.

Edward Agreed. Tired of it myself. And the sniping. The moment you've said it, you wish you hadn't said it, but it's too late, you've said it, it's said.

Robert So why not quit?

Edward It takes years of training really successfully to grumble, but yes, I will, I'll stop.

Robert When?

Edward When there's nothing left to grumble about.

Robert You are coming over in the summer?

Edward I am. You get yourselves established and –

Robert What'll you do till then?

Edward Nothing I can do, except sit and write verse. I've no other work. (*Cheerfully.*) So we'll probably starve.

Robert Your new ones are good. 'Aspens'. That's good. 'Wind and Mist'. Good.

Edward Thanks. That means a lot.

Robert produces a letter.

Robert I heard from Chicago. *Poetry Magazine* want to take six of your pieces. Fall issue.

Robert gives the letter to Edward, who is delighted.

Edward But that's tremendous news! (*Calls.*) Helen! (*Reading the letter.*) How marvellous!

Robert Look, you should drop the pseudonym: you're not Edward Eastaway, you're Edward Thomas, be proud of your –

Edward No, I can't do that –

Robert Why don't you come now? To Franconia? You'll still get a berth. We'll take up the farm together!

Edward Rob, I'm not a farmer. I wouldn't have a clue what to do!

Robert That doesn't matter! The whole point of farming is shirking your duties!

Edward Is it?

Robert Sure! How do you think I get any writing done?

They laugh. An awkward pause.

Edward A while ago I dreamt we were walking near Dymock, but we lost one another in a strange place, and I woke saying to myself, 'Some day I shall be here again.'

Robert Sounds like the last line of a poem.

Edward That's quite a coincidence. I think it is.

Another laugh, another pause.

Well –

Robert I'm not going to miss you at all.

Edward No, I'm not going to miss you either.

Robert But I never met anyone quite like you.

Edward No, I'm sure you didn't. Yankee poets, on the other hand –

Robert Yeah, ten-a-penny on the Charing Cross Road –

They embrace clumsily, briefly, and pull apart, embarrassed.

OK, where's the kid?

Edward (*calls*) Helen!

SCENE FOURTEEN

Night. Wind in the trees. Eleanor is alone. She has a lantern.

Eleanor (*to us*) The spring of 'fifteen was all dark rain and sopping mist. The war hadn't ended by Christmas, as many had thought that it would. I was well wrapped up and not expecting trouble. I had a clean hankie and a butterscotch. But events took a terrifying turn!

Helen enters, looking for the lantern.

Helen Eleanor?

Eleanor Over here! Coo-ee!

Helen Where is he?

Eleanor I'm just waiting as instructed, dear.

Helen On Shoulder-of-Mutton in the middle of the night?

Eleanor Looks like it!

Helen Do you always do as you're told?

Eleanor Well, if Edward tells me, yes.

Helen Why?

Eleanor (*giggling*) Because he's Edward!

Helen So you obey Edward. And he obeys me.

Eleanor Does he?

Helen I gather you've been looking over his new poems.

Eleanor Yes, I've been typing them out for –

Helen And have you been making corrections?

Eleanor I've been making suggestions, which –

Helen Well, don't.

Eleanor But he seems to appreciate –

Helen Eleanor? Don't. They're perfect as they are.

Eleanor (*to us*) They weren't.

Edward enters.

Edward Right, you two follow me. This way!

Edward forges ahead, stealthily. They follow him up through the woods.

Eleanor (*whispers*) Where's he taking us?

Helen The heart of ancient Albion.

Eleanor Gracious! How thrilling!

Edward Shh! Don't move!

They stand still and listen. The leaves rustle, the rain patters.

Now! (*Whispers.*) Stay very still. Hear it?

Helen Yes, I can! Oh!

Eleanor Oh! – What is it?

Helen A nightingale.

Edward The first of the year.

And now we hear, deep in the woods, the distinctive call of the nightingale.

Eleanor Oh, it's lovely!

Edward Isn't it?

Eleanor What a beautiful song! How happy he must be!

Edward Actually no. He's got six weeks to attract a mate, then the breeding season's over. The poor chap's desperate, in fact.

Helen But we are happy. That's what matters. Aren't we, Edwy? (*To Eleanor.*) We're planning our trip to America.

Eleanor (*surprised*) Oh, are *you* –

Helen (*to Edward*) Come and kiss me, show Eleanor how happy we are.

Eleanor Oh!

Eleanor giggles. Edward is embarrassed in front of her.

Edward Helen –

Helen How happy we'll be when we get to America.

Edward Please –

Helen Kiss me. Kiss your wife. Kiss me.

Edward I don't think –

Helen Kiss me, damn you.

Edward takes Helen in his arms and kisses her. She grips his hair and pulls his head to hers. Eleanor looks the other way.

Now kiss Eleanor.

Edward I have absolutely no intention of kissing Eleanor.

Helen I'm telling you to. Kiss Eleanor.

Edward This is rude and immodest.

Helen Why? No one's looking, we're up a bloody hill. Kiss Eleanor. She wants you to!

Eleanor (*giggling*) Gracious, I –

Edward No.

Helen Edward, I'm giving you an order.

Edward Helen, this is utterly –

Helen (*furiously*) Kiss her! Do it!

There is a pause during which the nightingale sings. Helen and Edward glare at each other. Helen means business.

Edward (*sighs*) Miss Farjeon, do you mind if I –

Eleanor Oh, goodness.

Edward pecks Eleanor.

Edward There. Done.

Helen Kiss her properly.

Edward Helen!

Helen Go on. Kiss her. I know you want to!

Edward This is craven!

Helen Kiss her on the lips!

Angrily, Edward takes hold of Eleanor and kisses her full on the lips. Eleanor swoons.

Oh! You did it! I know I said to but oh!

Horrified, Helen runs off into the woods.

Edward Helen! – Excuse me, Eleanor, sorry.

Edward runs off after her. Eleanor is left holding the lantern, somewhat dazed.

Eleanor (*to us*) I had never kissed a man in the whole of my life! Apart from my brother of course, when he was Launcelot and I was Guinevere, or I was Thisbe and he – well it was entirely indescribable! I've read many attempts to describe it and they're all wide of the mark! It's electric! And yet it's only one's lips, only the lips that touch, only the blood in the lips! How can lips alone do that to one? Honestly, I thought I was going to faint!

Let me have a breather. A girl can only take so much.
Edward was killed at the Battle of Arras on the ninth of April, nineteen seventeen. He was standing by his unit when a late shell came over, and that was the end of that. Dear Edward. He counted on me for friendship, and I loved him with all my heart.

SCENE FIFTEEN

Edward enters in his walking clothes, knapsack on his back. He waves desperately to someone just ahead of him.

Edward Please, stop! Will you stop? Stop! I just want a word. One word!

The person in the distance must have stopped, as Edward now doffs his hat, puffing.

Thanks. Look: I am trying to become a conscious Englishman. I am trying to step out of the dream, and into my life. I have been longing for catastrophe, for something to change, something to break – and here it is, here's the crisis, here's the shove in the back. But I'm just a writer! I write books! What is a chap supposed to do?
Oh, you're laughing? Is it funny? Yes, all right, it's funny. I am a joke, I know that. I run from a fight, I know that. I am tainted, but I would be cleansed.
And you are the Other Man – no, don't deny it. You go before me, and you come after. Tell me what to do. Tell me, please! How can I be true to myself, and also true to my country? (*He listens.*) Really? It's as simple as that?

He is overcome with relief.

Is that all? Really? (*A big smile.*) Thanks.

Fade out.

Act Two

SCENE SIXTEEN

Hampstead. The sounds of a party. Eleanor enters in evening dress, with a cocktail, and an olive on a stick.

Eleanor (*to us*) In some cultures they say that when you see your double you have met your death. Robert Frost told me that. Robert Frost . . . After our summer in Dymock, I didn't see him again for forty-two years. Didn't hear a word. But when he passed through London in the 'fifties, he came up to Hampstead to tea, and we had a super time. By then I'd made a minor name for myself, with my Martin Pippin, my Jenny Dove – oh, nothing like the celebrity of Frost! – but we shared common ground nonetheless: we were both still obsessed with dear Edward. I was then writing my memoir of him, and Robert had championed his work in the United States. And so we talked, and reminisced, and conjured Edward, whom we both worshipped in our disparate ways, and it was as if the forty-two years had never been, the forty-two years of silence. They'd been hard times for Robert. He had suffered much loss. But he bore up well. He didn't manage to visit Mrs Thomas on that trip, something prevented it, but he left me with an abiding memory of his manly love for our dear, dear friend, who famously dillied and dallied – until one day his path became clear.

SCENE SEVENTEEN

Petersfield. Helen, in her work clothes, is digging in the garden, her fork clagged with mud. July 1915.

Helen (*sings under her breath*)
I know where I'm going
And who's going with me
I know who I love
But the devil knows who I'll marry.

Edward (*off*)
I know where I'm going
And who's going with me –

Delighted, Helen tries to clean herself up in the moments before Edward enters. When he does, he is wearing the uniform of a private in the Artists' Rifles. No weapons. He's cheerful.

Good evening!

Helen is stunned.

I've enlisted.

Helen remains speechless.

I passed the medical.

Helen What?

Edward Remarkably, I passed!

Helen You were going up to look for work! Not to –

Edward It was an impulse. Well, an impulse I've been considering. A considered impulse.

Helen That's a decision!

Edward So it is.

Helen Edward, tell me exactly what you've done.

Edward I caught a bus to Euston this morning. I walked into the headquarters of the Artists' Rifles. I attested. I have three days to fix my affairs, then I report for training. There's nothing to worry about, Helen, it's all –

Helen I'm not *worried*!

Edward Then why are –

Helen I'm *appalled*! This is absolute madness! You don't have to join the Army!

Edward I know I don't have to –

Helen You're meant to be clever!

Edward Everyone has to do their bit, it's –

Helen Your bit isn't this bit, yours is a different bit, it isn't this! You're meant to be going to America! To Merfyn! To Frost! To milk cows!

Edward I have to serve my country, d'you see? Once I had realised that, I –

Helen Christ! You can serve your country in a multitude of ways! Other ways!

Edward No. I can't. I have to make the gesture.

Helen Damn it to hell, Edward, I've seen you make some stupid gestures in my time, but this one takes the biscuit! It's not our war! It's theirs! It's the King and the Kaiser and their bloody silly cousins! It's nothing to do with us!

Edward If I can't fight for my country I don't deserve to live in it.

Helen But what do you think you are fighting for? What? Belgium? A principle? What?

Edward picks up a handful of soil, and lets it run through his fingers.

Edward This, literally this.

Helen Why, why, why, why, why? Why do men love to fight?

Helen weeps miserably.

Edward I don't know why.

Pause.

I slept well last night. I felt peaceful.

Helen Peaceful? That's a good one!

Edward Helen, there are men and boys over there having a rough time, a rotten time, for us. Either I've never loved England, or I've loved England blindly, like a slave, like an automaton, a nine-to-fiver, a railway commuter. Why should we leave it to others to fight our battles? Why?

Helen Who have you talked to about this?

Edward Well, Eleanor –

Helen Naturally, Eleanor, and –

Edward And the Other Man. I've talked to him.

Helen Oh, Christ. Edward –

Edward I need to go. It's as simple as that.

Helen Edward, there is no Other Man. It's in your imagination! Oh, what am I going to do with you?

Edward There is an Other Man.

Helen Right.

Edward There is. I've seen him.

Helen Right. – So you're heading off –

Edward In three days, yes, report to camp. Epping Forest, rather a nice part of Essex.

Helen And what will I tell them at Bedales?

Edward I don't care a fig for Bedales.

Helen Edward, everything I have is here, in this village, at the school, and the children – (*Wails.*) Oh, I don't understand!

Edward Nor do I understand. But I do love you, Helen, and I know you love me, and this is what I have to do, and you simply have to trust me.

He's very calm. A pause. Helen sits down disconsolately.

I'll probably be the oldest fellow in the battalion.

It's an attempt at a joke but it only brings more tears.

Helen Oh, Edward . . .! You utter fool!

Edward kneels and puts his arm around her.

Edward Don't cry, old girl.

Helen Life is too hard, it's too hard –

Edward It has been hard, I know.

Helen So that you could write and we could live in the country, we've been through such –

Edward I know we have. I know. But it hasn't – it hasn't been such a poor existence, has it? Has it really?

Helen (*snuffles*) It's a long way from Wandsworth, I'll give you that.

Edward I don't expect I shall see action. They have fit, brave chaps for that, chaps not scared of gamekeepers. But there's no going back. I'm a soldier.

Helen These clothes . . . they're so awful . . . so scratchy and stiff.

Edward The boots pinch vilely, to be honest. (*Beat.*) Helen, I'll be paid, they will send you my wages.

Helen But what about your –

Edward I shan't need anything. I'll be in camp.

Helen Oh, God.

Pause.

Please tell me it will be over quickly.

Edward Six months, I expect, six months.

Helen Yes . . .

Edward If I get to France at all I'll be lucky.

He's said the wrong thing again. There's a pause.

Helen You said you loved me.

Edward Yes, I did. I don't know quite how that happened.

Helen It was nice.

Helen leans in and kisses him, and he responds.

Let's go for a walk. Shall we?

Edward The children –?

Helen Oh, rot the children. There are days when I hate the bloody children.

Edward (*laughs*) Where shall we go?

Helen Up Shoulder-of-Mutton. Come on.

Helen pulls him up, and they go off holding hands. We see Eleanor.

Eleanor (*to us*) He became a poet on the way to war. What a shame that he didn't live to see any of his verse published under his own name. What a rotten shame.

I was very close to Edward and I could have . . . I could have . . . and now everything has changed. The whole country has changed. Once we had a maypole on every village green. Now we have war memorials.

Sometimes the ship sails by. Quite often in my case. Men are a mystery, aren't they?

From offstage, a man's voice calls: 'Nellie! I say!'

(*To us.*) I should be in there with my guests. I shouldn't be talking to you. Excuse me, I must go.

We hear laughter and chatter and the chink of glass. Eleanor heads towards it, then turns back:

I hope you will never be as wretched, as lonely as I am tonight.

Eleanor exits to the party.

SCENE EIGHTEEN

Robert is on the verandah of his farm in Franconia, New Hampshire. When he writes, he sits in his favourite chair, his writing board on his knee.

Robert (*to us*) We came home on the *St Paul*, in convoy with the *Lusitania*, and made our way from Boston to Franconia Notch. Two months later the *Lusitania* was torpedoed, and a thousand people died. But I wasn't among them. Perhaps I shall live a long time.

My grandfather bought me my first farm – poetry was always a beggar – but I bought this. And you know what? When they heard who I was, they put the price up! How do you like that?

He slits open an envelope. As well as a handwritten letter, there are several typed sheets of poems, which he takes out.

My buddy wrote me every few days. From England at first, then France. (*Chuckles.*) Who woulda ever thought he would so enjoy soldiering?

SCENE NINETEEN

Edward, in uniform, now sporting a lance-corporal's stripe, is with his father Philip in the family home in Clapham. Late 1915.

Philip A map-reading instructor? You're to be a map-reading instructor?

Edward Yes, I suppose because I'm good at reading maps!

They laugh together.

Philip I suppose so! – Then will they not want you in France?

Edward I don't know. I've been accepted for officer training. So probably they will.

Philip Good show! Edward, that is grand. You'll take a sherry?

Edward I don't usually – but –

Philip Oh, you will. Celebration!

Edward Very well, a small one.

Philip pours drinks. They are not exactly generous.

Philip If you knew how delighted I am.

Edward I'm pleased that you're pleased.

Philip My son, an officer. Well there is a wonder. A miracle, as you might say.

Edward Yes, isn't it? One day I'll command a battery of six-inch Howitzers, but for now we mainly hike across Hampstead Heath and draw what are called 'panoramas'. It's not bad work.

Philip Well I am proud of you, whatever it is. Your good health.

Edward Thank you. Cheers.

Philip Fiercely proud.

Edward (*smiling*) That makes me – well, you know.

Philip Now, there are certain practicalities we must discuss, if you are to be billeted here. Your mother has somehow got into her head the notion that you are a vegetarian.

Edward Well, yes, I have to –

Philip No, no. I have six sons, and not one of my sons is vegetarian.

Edward I am, actually, father. I have a recurring digestive –

Philip But the sight of you in uniform! Looking spruce! That is a treat for an elderly man.

Edward Thank you, I've nearly got used to the –

Philip Haircut soon, I think?

Edward I'm due at the barber's on Monday.

Philip And your woman?

Edward My wife? Helen?

Philip She will be coming here?

Edward No, she's at Petersfield, with the children. Every couple of weeks, I'll go home, I'll get leave.

Philip She'll stay in Hampshire. Splendid. And how are you finding the Artists' Rifles? I suppose I shall have to forgive you not joining a Welsh regiment!

Edward Nothing to complain about, so far. Discipline. Routine. One doesn't have to think. Just – you know – spit and polish.

Philip That is the spirit, Edward, that is the spirit. Give them the cold steel.

Edward And you are looking well, Father.

Philip I am well, very kind of you to say so. My leisure hours are full. They flatter me that I am the lynchpin of the Battersea Ethical Society.

Edward I don't doubt it.

Philip Positivism. That's the new thing. Comtean positivism. Watch us change the world! – But look at you in khaki. By God I am impressed!

Edward beams with pleasure.

We will smash the Prussian swine, soon enough.

Edward Come now, I don't think we need refer to them as –

Philip Get out and blow them to the devil, as many as you can!

Edward Father –

Philip They are bayoneting little children, women they are chopping up for fun!

Edward You mustn't believe everything you read in the newspapers. It's propaganda.

Philip It is not propaganda, they are German –

Edward I doubt the Germans are much different from us.

Philip Different from us? Of course they are different from us, they are for a start Teutonic –

Edward Yes, all right, but they're not sub-human –

Philip They are barely men at all! The Hun are cowards, they are frightened of cold steel! Everyone knows that!

Edward I'm sure our chaps are just as frightened as their chaps, if truth be told –

Philip (*very angry*) Nonsense! Total nonsense! Our troops are brave!

Edward Father, I am a patriot, but –

Philip You sound to me excessively pro-German!

Edward I'm not pro-German! But we're not fighting their entire race, are we?

Philip Why not? Wipe them out! Wipe them off the earth! The Teuton fuckers!

Edward (*shocked*) Father! – Please, try to understand. I'll go to the war – I'll fight – but I don't have to hate the German people. I will never hate the German people.

Philip You could be arrested, you know, for talking like that –

Edward Oh, could I?

Philip Oh yes, we have the Defence of the Realm Act, precisely for nancy-boys like you!

Edward Now there are laws against thinking.

Philip Look, are you capable of rational debate or are you not? You, with all that schooling? For what have you joined up, if you don't want to kill Germans?

Pause.

The floor is yours.

Edward To do my duty.

Philip And what is that?

Edward I'm not sure, it's rather complic—

Philip Then let me tell you! It is to kill the enemy, slaughter them, bomb them till there are none left!

Edward No!

Philip Good grief! – What a waste of an officer training.

Edward Thanks. I knew it was too good to last.

Philip Of course it was too good to last. Everything about you is too good to last. It was too good to last when you were winning the walking race. You were in sight of the finish and you stopped. I have never forgotten it. Why the devil, Edward, had you to stop?

Edward I thought I heard footsteps behind me.

Philip Of course you heard footsteps behind you! There were thirty-odd boys in the race!

Edward No – I heard another. Coming close.

Philip You were yards in front! – and you funked it. And this has been your long suit, ever since. Oxford. The Civil Service. Books. I look at you now, and I see a man who has failed. I see a man who could have bettered himself, like his brothers have done, could have had a position, paid holiday, superannuation –

Edward I have started writing poems!

Philip Hip hip hooray.

Edward Thirty, forty poems!

Philip And how much have you earned from that? Idiot.

Edward feels weak. He trembles.

Edward You have always made me feel very small . . . ashamed to be alive.

Philip Putting on a uniform does not make you a man.

SCENE TWENTY

Robert on his verandah. He reads the typewritten sheaves of poems from Edward. He whistles through his teeth with admiration.

Robert 'Blessed are the dead that the rain rains upon.'

These are not poems about war. Edward never mentions the trenches. But they are poems engendered by war, the pressure of war, the expectation of war, the crushing weight of the present forcing up a stream of lava from the past, yeah, hot lava, primal matter, from deep beneath the crust of the man. The real thing. Simply thrilling.

He reads another page.

'Or must I be content with discontent
As larks and swallows are perhaps with wings?'

Boy . . .!

Got any idea how difficult it is to do what he's doing? How technically difficult? He plays with rhythm and line-length like a master, yet he's only been at it eighteen months. I've been trying twenty years and I . . . Well, put it this way: the guy sure is raising the stakes!

Robert folds the sheets of paper and puts them in his pocket.

He shipped out to France in early 'seventeen.

SCENE TWENTY-ONE

France, March 1917. Artillery in the background. Edward enters the office of Major Lushington, in a ruined chateau. He salutes. He wears his oilskin and filthy wellington boots. Lushington, his CO, is slightly younger than Edward. Edward salutes.

Edward Second Lieutenant Thomas, 244 Battery, sir!

Lushington At ease, Edward.

Edward Sir!

Lushington You've been up to Beaurains?

Edward Yes, I've reconnoitred potential Observation Posts.

Lushington Your maps are first class.

Edward Thank you, sir.

Lushington What did you want to see me about?

Edward Sir, I've been in France for two months. All that time I've been seconded to Heavy Artillery HQ, supervising camouflage and digging in.

Lushington Colonel Witchall is pleased with your work. You're efficient. Wish we had more men like you.

Edward Thanks, but – I don't want to remain an Adjutant – I want to get up to the line. I should be with my battery. I am requesting a transfer.

Lushington Edward. The men look to you as a father.

Edward Well, I am a father, sir.

Lushington I mean you are a popular figure, with your clay pipe and your books. You're eccentric. It cheers them up to see you.

Edward Thank you, sir.

Lushington If I send you up to the Forward OP, you'll be killed. Do you have a death wish, Edward?

Edward No, Major. I don't.

Lushington Then could you possibly explain to me this foolhardy request?

Edward I am rather impatient to go out and be shot at.

Lushington I see.

Edward That's why I came to France.

Lushington I see.

A shell lands nearby and they instinctively duck.

Edward All I want is to *do* something, d'you see, if I am discovered to be of any use –

Lushington But you are of use! Supervising the camouflage and the –

Edward But I'm fed up of sitting on my arse!

Lushington Look, you have worked on the drawings! You know what's planned for Easter Monday. There will be the dickens of a barrage!

Edward And we are both aware, Major, that good ground observation is essential for that barrage – and that's what I excel at.

Lushington Edward, you are thirty-nine years old. You have a wife and children. You could have stayed a map instructor. You could have stayed at home. But you've come out. Now you're here, you could sleep in a safe billet. The Colonel loves your panoramas! You don't have to go up the line! Consider it for a minute. Do you still want to request this transfer?

Edward Yes, sir.

Lushington I think you have a death wish. Dismiss.

Edward salutes and exits.

SCENE TWENTY-TWO

Robert on his verandah.

Robert Many of my Faculty colleagues think he had a death wish. They ask me, after lectures, why did he do what he did? People find it enigmatic, but to me it's plain. He did what he did because he was a man. And a man's got to walk through the woods.

Look, he was on poor terms with his father, and poor terms with his son. That's not unusual. I don't see eye to eye with my own boy. But also, Thomas's marriage was dead in all but name – there was a woman in Essex, that I think he adored. He kept real quiet about that. And his career was going nowhere. His books – they didn't sell. They were no use as travel guides – they were quite simply maps of his soul!

Look, he has to test himself, he has to prove to himself that he's the person he wants be. Prove something to the father, if you wish, but that sounds like another ism to me, and I don't care toffee for Mr Freud, I leave that to the lady professors, of whom there are now quite a few.

So the man walks on, into the dark, under the canopy of leaves, in some ritual of passage that is outside time. But every man's forest is different, and nobody's path is the same. For me the test, the battle, was to make myself a man of letters, and having made myself one, to remain one all my days. Like I say, everyone's different.

Edward comes out of a dug-out at his Forward OP on the front line. He wears his oilskin, silk scarf and helmet. His clay pipe is in his mouth, unlit. He takes off his helmet and lays it aside. He has a pair of field glasses which he raises to his eyes. He sweeps the glasses slowly round the horizon. In the distance we hear the thud of artillery, and now and then an aeroplane goes over.

Edward Well, how-do-you-do . . .

Edward lowers the glasses and takes out his field notebook.

Sparrow-hawk over No-Man's-Land; he's just taken a mouse. Beautiful cloudless morning. No firing yet. Drew a panorama at seven. Linnets and chaffinches singing in the trench. Four or five aeroplanes hovering and wheeling, as the kestrels used to over Mutton and Ludcombe.

Edward makes an entry in his notebook, then takes up the field glasses again.

Upon my word, he's just caught another one! The mice must be travelling today.

(*To us.*) My dear Robert – You don't write. Why not? We are having many fine days, bright and warm even at times. The hedge I spy through is of elder – chaffinches sing nearby and larks hover just in front – but my hedge is the only one, for as far as I can see. Everything else is gone.

I only live now in the hours when I can smoke. Sometimes all through a wet, cold night I do not live, I only smoke. I read Shakespeare for ten minutes every evening before blowing my candle out.

Long hours of waiting. Nothing that has to be done and yet not free to do what I want, in fact not consciously wanting anything except, I suppose, the end. Wisdom perhaps trickles in, perhaps not. I rather inhibit introspection, except when I wake up and hear the shelling, and wonder if I should move my bed away from the wall. I wasn't going to take a commission, but Helen will get a more substantial pension, d'you see? Have my verses been published in the States? I should like to be a poet, just as I should like to live – but I know as much about my chances in either case, and I don't really trouble about either. – Rob, the barrage has started up, I must go now to my battery.

Edward fastens on his helmet and exits as the barrage quickly begins to build. The steady thud now of heavy artillery.

Robert (*reads the letter*) 'Things will happen that will trample and pierce, but I shall go on, something that is here and there like the wind, something unconquerable, something not to be separated from the dark earth and the light sky, a citizen of infinity and eternity. My dearest love to you all . . .'

And from my porch in Franconia, the White Mountains a-gleam through the firs, it seemed that I could hear those frightful guns.

Robert folds up the letter and exits. The barrage becomes deafening. It grows dark. Just the distant flash of the heavy artillery.

SCENE TWENTY-THREE

The blast of a huge explosion. Edward is pitched up into the air and falls to earth in a crumpled heap. He doesn't stir. It grows quiet, and then there is the faint sound of birdsong. Edward opens his eyes.

Edward Is it over?

He sits up. There is no blood, but he doesn't look very lively.

I think that was a four-point-two. (*Gazing around.*) Are you there? I can't see you.

Pause.

Have you gone? Is it over?

He stands, a lone figure against the desolate landscape of No-Man's-Land. The birdsong increases minimally.

(*To us.*) Has anyone seen the Other Man?

He comes towards us, relaxed and happy.

I think he's gone. Of course he's gone. He's gone!

He stands still, content, and listens to the birds. He smiles at a pleasant memory,

All the birds of Oxfordshire and Gloucestershire.

SCENE TWENTY-FOUR

Petersfield. Helen and Eleanor, both wearing black armbands. A parcel has just been delievered and they have cut the string. May 1917.

Eleanor Be brave.

Helen I'm fine. Let's see what we've got.

They unwrap the parcel.

Save the string.

They take out the contents one by one. They are Edward's possessions, returned with a letter from the Front. First out are his letters and diary containing a photo of Helen, then a compass, dividers, a pencil case.

His prismatic compass. Did you buy that?

Eleanor nods. Next Helen takes out a small book.

Shakespeare's *Sonnets*. He used to read these to me. Look, Eleanor. The pages are all creased –

Eleanor How strange –

Helen – as if they'd been taken out, and screwed up –

Eleanor – and ironed flat and put back.

Helen The inventory says that it was in his pocket when he died. Did I tell you, it was the shock of the blast that killed him? – There were no external wounds.

Eleanor Can a shell do that?

Helen The concussion, isn't it?

Eleanor I don't know.

Helen Oh! His pipe.

Helen takes out the clay pipe and a tin of York River tobacco.

York River.

She opens the tin and smiles.

The smell of it in the house . . . It always meant my darling had come home.

Helen snuffles. Eleanor comforts her. Helen composes herself.

I'm all right. Thanks. – Shall we put this in a case, and stand it on the mantel?

Eleanor Oh! – that's a good idea. So Bronwen and Merfyn and Myfanwy can –

Helen Yes. Lay it down gently. I don't want it to break.

Helen takes out another small book.

Eleanor It's Robert's new collection. Edward said he had got that.

Helen Did he?

Eleanor He said he was the only man in the trenches who'd read it.

Helen *Mountain Interval.* Well, he's up on his mountain. We're down on the plain.

Eleanor May I see?

Eleanor takes Mountain Interval *and turns to the first line of the first poem.*

(*Reads.*) 'Two roads diverged in a yellow wood' – sounds like Robert.

Helen Could be either of them.

Eleanor (*laughs*) It could. (*Reading on.*) This one's *about* Edward, I think.

Helen breaks down and weeps.

Helen Oh, why did he have to go? The stupid man!

Eleanor There, there, dear.

Helen Tell me what you remember. Tell me everything. How did you meet him? Tell.

Eleanor He used to play cricket with Bertie.

Helen How he loved his cricket!

Eleanor He was frightfully absent-minded on the pitch. He dropped a lot of catches. Neither could he bat.

Helen He loved his cricket, Eleanor.

Eleanor Oh yes. And he loved his walking. I used to call him Walking Tom. How we used to laugh!

Helen takes back the book and lays it with the other things.

Helen Yes, I know you made him laugh.

Eleanor And so did you, I'm sure!

Helen No.

Eleanor Oh but you must have!

Helen Eleanor. I have always known.

Eleanor What have you always known, dear?

Helen About you and Edwy.

Eleanor What about myself and Edwy, Helen?

Helen About your feelings for him.

Eleanor is stunned but doesn't deny it. There's a silence.

I thought the thing to do was draw you in. Make friends with you. Keep watch. But now I've got to know.

Eleanor (*weakly*) Don't say we're not friends any more.

Helen You've got to tell me. I've got to know.

Eleanor There's nothing to tell!

Helen He's dead, Eleanor!

Eleanor Yes, and we both wish he wasn't! Helen – please!

Helen Tell me the truth, the truth about you and Edward!

Eleanor There's nothing to tell!

Helen Were you lovers?

Eleanor (*shocked*) Helen!

Helen Were you lovers? Were you and my husband lovers?

Eleanor No, never, never! I'd never do a thing like that!

Helen But he might?

Eleanor I don't know! No, of course not! Edward was a gentleman!

Helen You're saying you never slept with him?

Eleanor Helen –

Helen You never went to bed with him? In Hampstead? Or here? Or in a haystack somewhere? Never?

Eleanor (*in tears*) There is no need to be so coarse!

Helen Tell me what happened! I've got to know!

Eleanor . . . Nothing. Nothing happened.

Helen But you loved him, didn't you?

A long silence.

Eleanor I loved him awfully.

Another long silence.

Helen You never went to bed with him?

Eleanor Helen, I've never been to bed with anybody.

Helen Do you expect me to believe that?

Eleanor I'm not like you!

Helen I think I'm going to go mad. Leave me alone. Let me go mad.

Eleanor Helen, shall I make you a cup of –

Helen No! Leave me alone! Get out of my house!

Eleanor I can't leave you so –

Helen Just get out of my house, Nell, just go! You're banished! Goodbye!

Eleanor Helen . . .?

Helen Goodbye!

Eleanor Helen . . .? Helen dear?

Helen steadfastly refuses to turn and face Eleanor.

SCENE TWENTY-FIVE

Robert alone. He wears an expensive new overcoat, an expensive new hat.

Robert (*to us*) I returned to England – sick and old – in nineteen fifty-seven. They had some honours that they wanted to bestow. By that time I'd gotten so many degrees, I'd had a patchwork quilt made out of them. But it was tough, that visit, going back to Dymock especially, because, of the folks that I'd had with me in 'fourteen, three were dead – my wife; my daughter Marjorie, in childbirth; my son, shot himself in Vermont – and my other daughter Irma, years in an asylum. I was alone. And it was hard, sitting there and thinking of Edward. When we met, I was a failure. I had failed at everything. I was the first-round draft pick who didn't pay out. And yet here was I now, garlanded, honoured, feted as a poet – and my poor friend – my great friend – was not.

I was besieged by his widow on that visit. I made arrangements to pay my respects, but when the moment came . . . I couldn't go. I couldn't face the woman. Could not sit and drink her tea. I told Eleanor Farjeon to cook up an excuse. It wasn't Helen that I wanted to remember. It was Edward. Helen I could go my ways without.

Because I had seen her in London, eleven years after the Battle of Arras – let's see – that's nineteen twenty-eight. The memory of that encounter has been painful ever since.

1928. Regent's Park. Helen waits in her shabby overcoat and hat. She looks grey and drawn, and damaged. She smokes hard. Robert approaches, looking prosperous.

Helen Robert, how nice to see you.

Robert Mrs Thomas.

Helen Oh you must call me Helen, I know we have business, but oh –

Robert How have you been, Helen?

He offers his arm. She takes it and they walk.

Helen I have had some trouble. With my nerves.

Robert I'm sorry to hear it. And the children? How are they?

Helen I don't know.

Robert Oh, gee.

Helen Eleanor's been wonderful.

Robert Eleanor Farjeon?

Helen Yes. She's never married, so she has plenty of time. Oh, she has gentleman friends, but they're all rather wet. I don't know why she goes to quite so much trouble for the children and myself. Guilt, I suppose.

Robert Would you give her my regards? (*Looks around, pleased with himself.*) Regent's Park. Who'd a guessed?

Helen You've certainly made your return in style.

Robert It's eleven years, Helen. Quite a lot has happened.

Helen Where's your wife?

Robert She's over in France. We've been on a lecture tour.

Helen Does she like France?

Robert No. See, we don't speak the language, and –

Helen I'm not sure Mrs Frost speaks any language, does she? She certainly never spoke mine.

Pause.

Why didn't you fight? Are you a coward?

Robert I was too old for the war.

Helen Nobody was too old for the war! Not in England, anyway!

Robert Helen, is it so bad *not* to die?

Pause.

Helen. Do we have to be enemies?

Helen I used to wish and pray to be different. I used to wish I was beautiful and wise. But I'm not beautiful and I'm not wise, and I have only one thing in my life, and that is the memory of Edward. And I cannot believe what I'm hearing from across the Atlantic. Is it true? You've cut me out?

Robert Your book was banned in Boston!

Helen Yes, and I'll go to my grave knowing that at least I did one thing in my life, as least I annoyed some bloody Catholics!

Robert Helen, Helen – I know you've had some –

Helen Episodes? Breakdowns? What word would you use? You're good with words.

Robert You've been unwell.

Helen I have been unwell. It helped me, to write my book. I wrote of my love for Edward, and life became possible again. Life. That old thing. – Is it true? What I'm told?

Robert Yes, it's true. I have removed the dedication from my *Selected Poems*.

Helen 'To Helen Thomas, in memory of Edward Thomas'?

Robert It will not be there in the new edition.

Helen (*upset*) I just wrote about Edward, what did I do?

Robert You insulted his manhood.

Helen I did what?

Robert You insulted his manhood, you wrote that he was – it pains me – that he was sexually inexperienced –

Helen Well, he was! You all were, once!

Robert There is a revolting passage where you describe your – intimacy on – where was it?

Helen Wimbledon Common.

Robert No gentleman should expect his wife to have to read that. The folks in Boston got it right. It's a shameful book! It makes him look ridiculous! A manly man would laugh!

Helen Why would a manly man laugh? What's wrong with men, that you would laugh? I am writing about his love for me, why would you laugh?

Robert Don't make me say it – Helen –

Helen Say it, you coward, say it –

Robert Look, I have talked to your husband. Long and hard. He was distinguished at Oxford for his repertoire of ribald songs – filth and promiscuity and –

Helen Oh, I've heard them all, Christ, I was married to him for Christ's sake –

Robert – and we all know he caught venereal disease from a streetwalker while –

Helen It was the relief of Mafeking! Everyone's defences were down! The whole of bloody Oxford was –

Robert – and that was why he got a poor degree!

Helen So? Who needs a degree? He was an artist!

Robert Helen, he was a *man*! Don't make him look like a pansy!

Helen You are too conventional for me, Robert. I have thought so ever since I caught you looking at me, the night when I danced in the barn.

Robert What do you mean, looking at you?

Helen Looking at my legs, looking at my arse! I saw that look!

Robert Gee, lady –

Helen You desired me! But you can't admit it to yourself. So you cast me as a whore. Hypocrite! You are, I think, the perfect ambassador for your revolting country.

Robert Forgive me, I got to go, you're unstable.

Helen But everything I wrote was true!

Robert Was it?

Helen Everything! Everything!

Robert And you are the sole guardian of the truth? The truth about Edward Thomas?

Helen I am his wife!

Robert But half of what you wrote is pure invention!

Helen I wrote a book, a whole book, that's more than you've ever done! With chapters! And paragraphs!

Robert OK. Listen. I'll see you.

He walks away, trying to control his anger. He turns back.

What you wrote – in one of your chapters – your last night together, before he went to France – you're telling me that's the truth? The truth, Helen?

Helen That was how it was.

Robert Well, it's not a guy I recognise. OK?

Helen That was how it was.

Robert It's not a credible description of a marriage!

Helen That was how it was.

Robert It's pure romance! Helen!

Helen That was how it was! That was how it was! That was how it was!

SCENE TWENTY-SIX

The Thomases' cottage. Dawn, 16 January 1917. Edward enters in his white long-johns. He carries a tray with a teapot, a strainer, two cups and saucers, milk and sugar. He carefully pours the tea. Helen enters in her nightgown, rubbing her eyes.

Edward Tea.

Helen How lovely.

Edward Let's not wake the children. I've said my goodbyes.

Helen Then let's not.

Edward (*kissing her tenderly*) I won't forget last night.

Helen You should dress. The train.

Helen sits and drinks her tea. Edward starts to dress, in layer upon layer of warm clothing.

Edward? I love you.

Edward Do you remember – when we made Merfyn?

Helen I remember every one of them. I remember what we did. Every time.

Edward What a girl!

Helen Don't go.

Edward I've got to go, my love. I've got to go. Bear up.

Helen starts to cry, softly. He continues to put on his uniform.

Helen Where did you get those woollens?

Edward Eleanor.

Helen Christ, how cold is it going to be? – You realise she's in love with you.

Edward No, she's not, she's from Hampstead.

Helen God, you're stupid!

Edward What have I done?

Helen (*suddenly cries out*) Don't leave me! Don't, please don't leave me!

Edward Sweetheart, sweetheart, be still. I will come back to you.

Helen (*through tears*) You'd better.

Edward I have to, I'm going to America. Franconia, the Northern Presidentials. Remember? How's the tea?

Helen It's sweet.

Edward Let me dress.

Helen watches as Edward dresses.
He works methodically. Sings softly.

O, my love is like a red, red rose,
That's newly sprung in June;
O, my love is like a melody
That's sweetly played in tune.
As fair art thou, my bonnie lass,
So deep in love am I –

Helen (*joining in*)
And I will love thee still, my dear,
Till all the seas gang dry.

Helen *and* **Edward**
Till all the seas gang dry, my dear,
And the rocks melt with the sun:
I will love thee still, my dear,
While the sands of life shall run.

And fare thee well, my only love
And fare thee well, a while!
And I will come again, my love,
Though it were ten thousand mile.

Helen helps Edward put on his revolver on the Sam Browne belt, and his greatcoat.

Edward That's the ticket.

Helen Will you write?

Edward Probably not. But tell Merfyn and Bronwen and Myfanwy that I love them, and they will be for ever in my thoughts.

Helen What about me? Will you forget me?

Edward Never. Never.

They kiss lingeringly.

Better go. The train –

Helen Yes, you had. Go on. Go.

Edward Helen, I'm sorry –

Helen For what?

Edward Not being a terribly good husband.

Helen I don't love you for your goodness. I love you for the badness *and* the goodness, the light and the dark, because it all makes you, and you have taken my heart and my body and my soul, and I shall never want them back again. Now go.

He swings his huge pack up on to his shoulder, and puts on his cap. He smiles at her and exits. She exits into the house, running. She runs back wearing her overcoat and gumboots. She goes to the garden gate.

Coo-ee!

Edward (*off*) Coo-ee!

Helen waits a while. We hear a train whistle in the distance. She waits, then calls again.

Helen Coo-ee!

Edward Coo-ee!

SCENE TWENTY-SEVEN

Robert, in summer walking clothes. He toys with a stick.

Robert (*to us*) Just three years and some I knew Edward – and we were together, in England, maybe only half that time. But I did feel I grasped him, knew him at his core. He was the brother I never had. I don't think he wanted to die, but he didn't want not to die. It took a war to bring him peace. He was an awkward fellow.

Yet I believed from the moment I first met him that he would someday clear his mind and save himself. So there is no regret – nothing I will call regret. Only I want to see him to tell him something. I want to tell him, what I think he liked to hear from me, that he was a poet. I want to talk endlessly with him still, either here in our mountains, or, as I find my longing is more and more, back in the woods of Gloucestershire, where first we talked of war.

Edward enters, in summer walking clothes. He's grumpy. We're back in Gloucestershire in 1914.

What's the matter today?

Edward My wife!

Robert What did you do?

Edward I lit my pipe, that's all.

Robert I sympathise with Helen.

Edward It's only a pipe!

Robert Shall we walk?

Edward Which way?

Robert May Hill?

Edward We could go to Ledbury?

Robert No. We'll go to May Hill.

They walk. Rooks call.

You ever think of other women?

Edward Why do you ask?

Robert The way you talk about your wife.

Edward Well . . . (*He thinks better of it.*) No.

Robert Uh-huh. Say – are they rooks or are they crows?

Edward Rooks.

Robert How do you tell the difference?

Edward If you see a rook on its own, it's a crow. If you see a lot of crows together, they're rooks.

Sings.

All round my hat, I will wear a green willow
All round my hat, for a twelve-month and a day
If anybody asks me the reason why I wear it
I'll tell them my true love is far, far away.

Robert That's pretty. What's the green willow stand for?

Edward It's a symbol of mourning.

Robert How so?

Edward I don't know. But I prefer it to Beethoven, just as I prefer any simple country church to Winchester or Gloucester Cathedral.

Robert Come on – that's perverse. Beethoven is better.

Edward Nonsense, total nonsense. Though the construction of folk song is straightforward, and the words are simple and direct, very often the meaning is complex, there are deep layers of nuance in the verse. One finds oneself stumbling over the rock strata of history. They are only the tales of wanderers, travellers on the road, but they hold as much knowledge as all of your Latin and Greek.

Robert It's not my fault I got Latin and Greek.

Edward It's not your fault you've got an annuity, either, is it?

Robert Hey, buddy? You're prickly today.

Edward Rob, I think I should enlist.

Robert No, you shouldn't enlist.

Edward I think I should. But I'll leave such a tangle behind me!

Robert Why do you want to enlist?

Edward My country's at war. I have a duty to fight.

Robert What? No, you – I thought you wanted to write poems?

Edward I want to try.

Robert First principle of the working poet: don't let anyone blow your head off.

Edward You might think differently if the USA was in the hostilities –

Robert The heck I would! Why would I? I'm not dying for the USA!

Edward Why not?

Robert I told you! I'm a poet!

Edward But we're at war!

Robert Ed! Let the other fellows go and get killed!

Edward Why? Why should they die and not me?

Robert That has to be the most specious, lunatic argument I have heard in a long, long while!

Robert snaps his stick.

Edward I wish you wouldn't do that!

Robert Do what?

Edward Snap sticks!

Robert Why not?

Edward It's irritating!

Robert It's irritating? You're irritating!

Edward I find you completely cynical, Robert –

Robert At least I can think for myself!

Edward Pardon?

Robert At least I'm not seduced by some muddle-headed notion of sacrifice, some semi-religious suicidal impulse posing as patriotic fervour!

Edward Excuse me, you are a guest here, and –

Robert It's politics, Ed, it's power, leave it to the other guys! We've got to think new thoughts!

Edward If you came from a place where history went back more than about a fortnight you might begin to understand the need to serve your country. Are you saying I'm wrong?

Robert No, I'm saying you're a sucker! You're a fool!

Edward Well I'm saying you're a self-serving, arse-licking Yank with eight hundred dollars a year! And now I'm going for a walk!

Robert Good!

Edward Goodbye!

Robert Goodbye!

They go in opposite directions.

SCENE TWENTY-EIGHT

Edward alone. He says his poem 'Lights Out'.

Edward

I have come to the borders of sleep,
The unfathomable deep
Forest where all must lose
Their way, however straight,
Or winding, soon or late;
They cannot choose.

Many a road and track
That, since the dawn's first crack,
Up to the forest brink,
Deceived the travellers
Suddenly now blurs,
And in they sink.

Here love ends,
Despair, ambition ends,
All pleasure and all trouble,
Although most sweet or bitter,
Here ends in sleep that is sweeter
Than tasks most noble.

There is not any book
Or face of dearest look
That I would not turn from now
To go into the unknown
I must enter and leave alone,
I know not how.

The tall forest towers;
Its cloudy foliage lowers
Ahead, shelf above shelf;
Its silence I hear and obey
That I may lose my way
And myself.

The End.

ACKNOWLEDGEMENTS

Extracts from Edward Thomas, *Letters to Helen* (Carcanet Press, 2000), copyright © Myfanwy Thomas, by kind permission of the Executor of the Estate of Edward Thomas.

Extracts from *The Letters of Edward Thomas to Jesse Berridge*, edited by Anthony Berridge (Enitharmon Press, 1983), by kind permission of the Executor of the Estate of Edward Thomas and Enitharmon Press.

Extracts from *Edward Thomas: The Last Four Years*, by Eleanor Farjeon (Sutton Publishing Limited, 1997) by kind permission of David Higham Associates.

Extracts from *Robert Frost: A Life*, by Jay Parini (William Heinemann, 1998), reprinted by kind permission of the Random House Group (UK) Limited and Jay Parini, c/o Markson Thoma Literary Agency, New York.

Extracts from *Into My Own: the English Years of Robert Frost, 1912–15*, by John Evangelist Walsh (Grove Press, New York), copyright © 1988 by John Evangelist Walsh, used by kind permission of John Evangelist Walsh and Grove/Atlantic Inc.

Extracts from *Elected Friends: Robert Frost and Edward Thomas to One Another*, edited by Matthew Spencer (Hansel Books, an imprint of Other Press, New York), copyright © 2003 Matthew Spencer, reprinted by kind permission of Other Press.

Extracts from *Under Storm's Wing*, by Helen Thomas (Carcanet Press, 1997), reprinted by kind permission of Carcanet Press.

Extracts from 'The Figure a Poem Makes', adapted from *Selected Prose of Robert Frost*, edited by Hyde Cox and Edward Connery Lathem, used by arrangement with Henry Holt and Company LLC, publishers, New York.

Extracts adapted from Frost letters to John T. Bartlett and Sidney Cox, from the book *Selected Letters of Robert Frost*, edited by Lawrence Thompson, used by arrangement with Henry Holt and Company LLC, publishers, New York.

'The Lesson for Today', as it appears in the authorised collection, *The Poetry of Robert Frost*, edited by Edward Connery Lathem.

Robert Frost quotation from *Newsweek*, 20 January 1956, used with the permission of the Estate of Robert Lee Frost.

With thanks to Peter Gilbert and the Robert Frost Estate; and to Richard Enemy and the Edward Thomas Estate.